Roar Like a Tiger

Story by Margaret Clough
Illustrations by Meredith Thomas

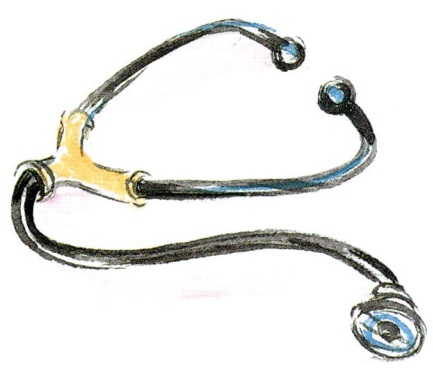

Katie said,

"Mum, my throat is sore."

"Come here, Katie," said Mum.
"I will look at your throat."

Mum said,

"Yes, Katie.

Your throat is very red.

We will go and see the doctor."

Mum and Katie and Joe went to see the doctor.

"Come here, please, Katie," said the doctor. "I will look at your throat."

"Mmm-mmm," said Katie.

"Come on, Katie,"
said the doctor.
"I can not see your throat."

"Mmm-mmm," said Katie.

"Please, Katie," said Mum.

Joe looked at Katie.

"I can roar like a tiger," he said.

"**Roar!**

Katie, can you roar, too?"

"I can roar," said Katie.

"**Roar!**"

"I like the way you roar, Katie," said the doctor.
"I can see all the way down your throat.
It looks red and sore."

"I can help a tiger with a sore throat," said the doctor.

"Thank you, Joe,"
said the doctor.
"Thank you for helping me."